The Garden Through the Year

PATIENCE STRONG

Frederick Muller Ltd
London

New Year's Morning in my Garden

On New Year's Day in the morning my
garden seemed to say—I know I'm not at my
brightest for the sky is bleak and grey. The
wind is cold and no birdsong ripples through
the leafless tree—but just below the earth
there lies a buried treasury—of sleeping bulbs
and dormant seeds. Just wait a month or two
—and many wonderful surprises I shall have
for you.

There'll be green tips thrusting through
and on your lawn you'll see—crocus carpets
yellow, purple, gold and ivory.

Flowers have Faces

Just like humans, flowers have faces with
expressions grave and gay. Some appear to
smile at you and others turn the other way ...
Some look pious and remote as if engaged in
secret prayer. Some look wild and frivolous
and others have a homely air.

Daisy faces, plain and simple. Pansy faces,
quiet and wise. Pale narcissi staring at you with
their rounded golden eyes. Poppy faces, boldly
painted. Lily faces, calm and white. Primrose
faces, fey, unearthly. Dahlia faces, broad and
bright ... Each one has its special meaning and
a message to convey. Each one has its place and
purpose and its little part to play. Though we
mass them into beds and crowd them in a tiny
space—Let us sometimes stoop and see the
beauty of each separate face.

The Breaking Bough

I thought the bough had broken when
upon the ground it lay—underneath a
weight of snow upon a bitter day—when
icy fingers gripped the branches of the
cedar tree, sparkling in the wintry sun:
a lovely sight to see ... But as I brushed
the snow away it sprang back into
place—stretching out a long green arm—
as if it would embrace—the glory of the
morning in the joy of gratitude—for
resuscitation, and for grace and strength
renewed.

Like the bough, an overburdened
mind can suddenly—sink beneath the
daily pressures of anxiety—but Faith
and Hope together working can relieve
the strain—and the drooping spirit be
restored to life again.

The Snowdrop

The ghost of a flower on a stalk thin and
green. Whiter than white it can scarcely
be seen—under the trees where the
grasses are glossed—with crystals of ice
and of sugary frost.

How did it get there and what made
it grow—thrusting a point through the
crust of the snow? How did it struggle
from out of its grave—that ghost of a
snowdrop, so eager and brave?

How did it know when to start on
its way—up through the dark to the
light of the day? The winds are still
bleak and the birds are still dumb—so
how did it guess that the moment had
come?

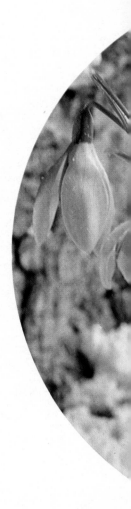

Earth

Fortunate you are if you possess a
patch of ground—in these days of
shortages and of a dwindling pound
... Even in a few square yards
you'd be surprised to see—what
you can produce to feed yourself
and family.

Never waste an inch of soil. It's
precious. Make it thrive. It is not a
concrete slab. It's earth and it's alive
... Keep on sowing, keep on
growing something you can eat.
Do your part with what you've
got to help to make ends meet.

The Holy Garden

Lententide is ending now, the long grey
wintry days—have brought us to the gates
of spring along the primrose ways—to
Holy Week; and step by step approaching
quietly we come unto the little garden of
Gethsemene. What is it to you, my friend?
Pause here to contemplate—the meaning
and the mystery—and to anticipate—the
miracle of your redemption. What is it
to you? Ask yourself this question. Is it
false or is it true? It if be a fable—Go
your way. Your pleasures take. Shed no
tears of penitence. No sacrifices make—
but if you have the courage to accept
this thing as true—You must face the
awful truth that Jesus died for YOU.

Perfect

Perfect are the lovely daffodils—arrayed in
bowls along my windowsills—with graceful
stalks and trumpets glowing gold—yet such
perfection somehow leaves me cold.

I cannot help but look beyond the pane—
to watch the wild ones swaying in the rain ...
Like ballerinas whirling in the breeze—to
blackbird-music from the apple trees.

My indoor beauties proud and stately
stand. The catalogue was right ... They're
really grand—and yet my heart they never will
entrance—because I like a daffodil to dance!

A Tapestry of Roses

Come lovely roses and set my garden glowing.
Open your buds. Too soon you will be going.
Make my small garden bright and beautiful.
This is your month: your own gay carnival.

Twine round the fence your pink and
crimson sprays. Line every path with glorious
blooms ablaze ... Hang on my wall a tapestry
of roses — that I'll remember when the summer
closes.

Life Flashes By

Midsummer Day has come and gone.
Slowly the sun now loses height.
Summer's rich splendour lingers on.
Roses still cluster, but day and night—the
glory is waning. The peak is passed. Time
makes its reckoning all too fast.

Life flashes by as we older grow.
Each passing year rushes swifter by.
Where do the runaway seasons go?
Vainly we wonder and question why—
but we can't bid the beautiful moments
stay—or call back one hour of a lovely
day.

Gather your memories secretly—so
you can dream when you are old—living
on Summer's legacy. Even though life
turn grey and cold—you will never feel
lonely, lost or sad—recalling the happy
times you had.

My Garden is My Kingdom

My garden is my kingdom. It's here
I'd like to spend—every hour the good
Lord gives from dawn till twilight's end—
but crowded are the busy days and rarely
can I spare—the time to work with fork
or spade—an odd hour here and there—
for can there be a greater pleasure under
heaven above—than working or at leisure
in the garden that you love?

Old Favourites

Sunflowers and michaelmas daisies come as the
summer grows old: commonplace flowers of
September, lavender, lilac and gold ... Year
after year in the borders of old fashioned
gardens they sprawl—when apples hang ripe in
the orchard and creepers flush red on the wall.

Needing no fuss or attention: just making
a wonderful sight—with patches of yellow and
purple gay in the autumn's soft light ... They
spread out in every direction and kindly con-
ceal from your view—the weeds you had no
time to gather, thus doing a good turn for you.

Catalogues showy and tempting more
up-to-date blooms may display—but let not old
friends be discarded and don't throw old favour-
ites away ... Somewhere in every new garden
—a corner I'd like to espy—for sunflowers and
michaelmas daisies to bid the old summer
goodbye.

Autumn Crocuses

They seem to take us unawares:
It's always a surprise — to see the
autumn crocus spearing up: a challenge
to the grey depression of the weepy
skies, the chalice of that lovely purple
cup.

The colour of the twilight when
the evening shadows steal—palest lilac
veined with snowy streaks. Strangers in
the garden, unfamiliar and unreal ...
Crocuses in autumn. Nature's freaks!

As if God had an afterthought and
summoned from the dead—the ghosts
of March to cheer us as we pass—the
phantom forms of spring uprising from
their earthly bed—before the frost lies
white upon the grass.

The Gardens in September

The gardens in September—how bright they are
and gay—outdoing in their splendour the
pageantries of May ... The asters bold and brilliant,
the dahlias rich and tall—The sunflowers in the
border, the creepers on the wall ... The gardens
of September, how beautiful they are—when
dawn with golden fingers puts out the morning
star. When fairy cobwebs glitter upon the dewy
lawn—and mists caught in the sunlight to silver
shreds are torn.

The gardens of September to Summer bid
goodbye. We know that we are watching the
year's last glory die—but there must be a winter,
a season cold and bare—a time of rest and
darkness for new life to prepare.

Manna in Winter

Every day in wintertime the birds come
flying round—waiting for the scraps that fall
like manna to the ground—When the cloth is
shaken out like magic they appear—and very
soon between them all the precious crumbs
they clear.

Many die of thirst and hunger in the bitter
time—when ice forms on the puddles and the
soil is sealed with rime. don't forget your
feathered friends. They'll thank you later on—
by singing at your window when the wintry
days have gone.

Underneath the Frozen Leaves

The brooks are black with glassy ice.
The woods are still and white—but underneath the frozen leaves, the wildflowers
out of sight—wait down in the darkness
for the moment to unfold. Celandines
and aconites will spread their pools of
gold—and the bracken with its sprays of
frosted crystal fronds—will beautify the
bridlepaths, the ditches and the ponds.

The years around us fade and fall
and settle silently—covering the past
beneath the leaves of memory—but
below the changing surface of our passing
days—lie the seeds that we have sown
along the hidden ways. Where our foot-
steps have been led, Lord, grant that
there may be—seeds of hope, of faith, of
friendship and of charity.

Never say that joy has fled forever
from your gate—because the winter of
your grief still lingers. Trust and wait.
Life lies dormant for a season. Keep
remembering—that underneath the
frozen leaves lie all the flowers of spring.

The Herald of the Heralds

The robin on the frosted holly sings
—to greet the month that brings the King
of Kings. This homely bird that haunts
my kitchen door—has wrought his
Christmas miracle once more.

His tiny throat has filled my garden
patch—with notes no human choristor
could match—in surpliced choir. Hear
now his sweetest chord: the herald
of the heralds of the Lord.